SHHH...

SHHH...

Song-Stretching Activities for Children's Favorite Tunes

Pamela Ott

Illustrations by Jordan Scott

CORWIN PRESS, INC.
A Sage Publications Company
Thousand Oaks, California

For information address:

Corwin Press, Inc.
A Sage Publications Company
2455 Teller Road
Thousand Oaks, California 91320
E-mail: order@corwinpress.com

SAGE Publications Ltd.
6 Bonhill Street
London EC2A 4PU
United Kingdom

SAGE Publications India Pvt. Ltd.
M-32 Market
Greater Kailash I
New Delhi 110 048 India

Printed in the United States of America

ISBN 0-7619-7544-6

This book is printed on acid-free paper.

00 01 02 03 04 05 10 9 8 7 6 5 4 3 2 1

Production Manager: Graphic Composition, Inc.
Cover Designer: Tracy E. Miller

Table of Contents

About This Book

In a child's day, there is a time for activity and a time for relaxation. Can you encourage this relaxation by playing calming music? You most definitely can. Have you noticed that doctors and dentists frequently play relaxing music in their offices to help keep us calm? Slow music calms children too. For years, mothers have sung lullabies to their children to help them fall asleep. Playing instrumental songs with a medium to slow tempo in the background helps set the pace for quiet time activities.

The *Shhh...* book contains a collection of activities that can be used on rainy days, or when quiet time activities are needed. It contains recipes, art activities, games, movement activities and science activities. *Shhh...* also contains sheet music for 15 calming pieces written or arranged by Pamela Ott. The recorded versions of these songs can be found on the accompanying *Shhh...* CD or audiocassette. These songs could also be played live on the piano or guitar.

This book was written with the intent of providing early childhood professionals, teachers and parents a collection of activities and ideas for those quiet times or rainy days. Recipes and activities can be varied to accommodate your students' ability levels. So — take a deep breath, relax, and enjoy!

How to Use This Book

This book is broken down into several sections. It begins with a section entitled "Quiet Time Activities." This section includes recipes for materials that can be used during a quiet time activity section. Following the recipes, there are sections on art activities, games, movement activities and science activities. Each new activity includes the materials needed and easy "how-to" instructions. Some activities contain additional ideas on expanding the concept presented.

The last section of the book contains "Quiet Time Music." This section contains the sheet music to 15 songs written or arranged by Pamela Ott. These songs can be played live on the piano, guitar or recorder. The recorded versions of these songs can be found on the accompanying *Shhh...* CD or audiocassette.

I recommend playing *Shhh...* or other calming music in the background as you participate in the activities listed in this book. Calming music really does help children (and adults) relax and slow down, allowing them to focus on the activity at hand.

Finally, be sure to make notes to yourself on what worked and on ideas that you may have while doing these activities that can be tried later.

About the Author

Pamela Ott started playing the piano and singing in elementary school. She credits the support and patience of two wonderful parents who put up with a lot of "beginning music sounds" and some caring music teachers in encouraging her to continue to develop her love of music by pursuing it as a career. She received her degree in Music Therapy from Colorado State University.

Pamela began to apply her musical skills to the creation of new educational music for children in 1980, and since then, her line of recordings and teaching manuals, "Teaching Tunes," has been used by teachers and early childhood professionals worldwide. She is a keynote speaker and workshop leader for many conferences nationally, and encourages the use of more music in the education of our children.

Pamela grew up in Colorado, but now calls Texas home, and lives there with her husband John and two children.

Quiet Time Activities

Recipes

The following are recipes for materials that can be used during a quiet time art session. Adults should monitor cooking activities carefully and should be sure to let students know that these recipes are not edible!

Fingerpaint

½ cup liquid starch
1 quart boiling water
½ cup liquid detergent
Tempera paint

Combine liquid starch and boiling water. Stir over heat until thick. Add liquid detergent. Stir. Put in small jars. Color with tempera paint. Store in the refrigerator. Remember that primary colors mix well to create other vibrant colors.

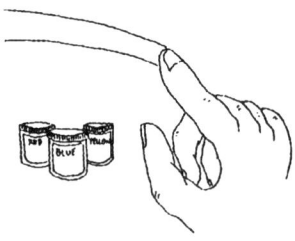

If you have the space and are willing to get messy, try toe and foot painting!

Playdough

This recipe makes a soft, pliable dough. It should stay fresh for a while if kept in an airtight container in the refrigerator.

1 cup flour
1 cup boiling water
1 tbsp. cooking oil
½ tsp. salt

To make your own playdough, combine flour, boiling water, cooking oil and salt. To color the playdough, add food coloring to the boiling water.

Saltdough

Saltdough can be air dried or sun dried to preserve the treasures you've created.

1 cup salt
2 cups flour
½ cup water

Combine flour, salt and ¼ cup of the water. Add a little more flour if the dough starts to stick to your hands. This dough usually air dries in 1 to 2 days unless it's very thick. Placing your dough in the sun can speed drying time.

Baker's Clay

This dough can be baked in the oven to a light brown and then colored or varnished.

1 cup salt
1 ½ cups warm water
4 cups flour

Stir salt into the warm water. Cool mixture, then add flour and knead for 10 minutes. To color the dough, add food coloring or ½ cup tempera paint to the salt and water mixture. Bake finished products at 300° for 1 hour. Thick pieces may require additional baking time.

Art Activities

This section contains ideas for art activities. You may wish to play the *Shhh...* CD or audiocassette quietly in the background as you participate in these activities.

Stamping or Block Printing

Stamp shapes for painting are frequently cut from sponges or potatoes, but there are many different objects that can be used. Go on a nature hike and collect materials that would make good stamps, such as leaves, rocks, wood, shells, bottle caps, or feathers. Dip these items in tempera paint and stamp them on a poster board or construction paper.

Try stamping a t-shirt or visor. Be sure to switch to a fabric paint (found in craft stores).

Rubs

Collect materials with varied textures, such as bark, leaves, coins, popsicle sticks, etc. Place them on a flat surface and cover them with a thin piece of paper. Using a peeled crayon, rub the side of the crayon gently over the paper until the shape of the object underneath begins to appear.

Scratch Art

Pieces of scratch art paper are available at many art supply stores. Scratch art paper is black on the outside, but when you scratch the black with a stick, rainbow colors appear below. Encourage children to try using different objects to scratch off their picture, as each object creates its own distinct look. Try a stick, a fingernail, a pen cap, etc. The best scratch object for the very young is a popsicle stick.

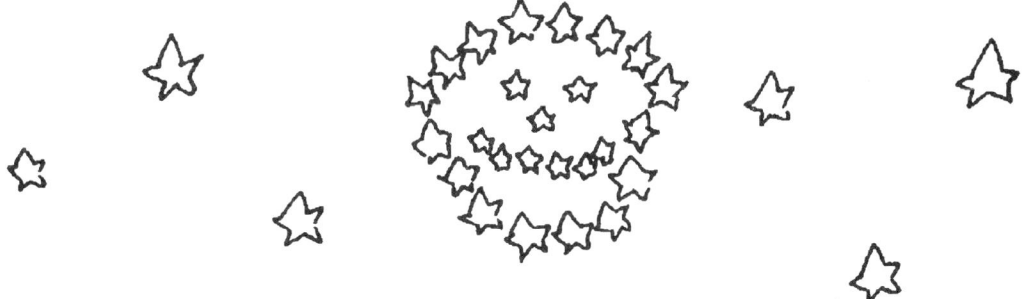

Constellations

Talk to your children about how ancient people used to think that the brightest stars in the sky created pictures, and so they named each one. Show them pictures of different constellations, such as Orion's Belt, and ask them if they can see the same picture that the ancient people did. Give your children a star pattern and have them cut out about 10 stars each. Give them each a large piece of butcher paper and ask them to create a constellation of their own. Hang these around your room for your own original night sky!

Melted Crayons

Gather small broken pieces of crayons from your art center. Put pieces of different colors in a paper cupcake cup. Place in the oven and melt crayons completely at a low heat while monitoring closely. Let cool and harden.

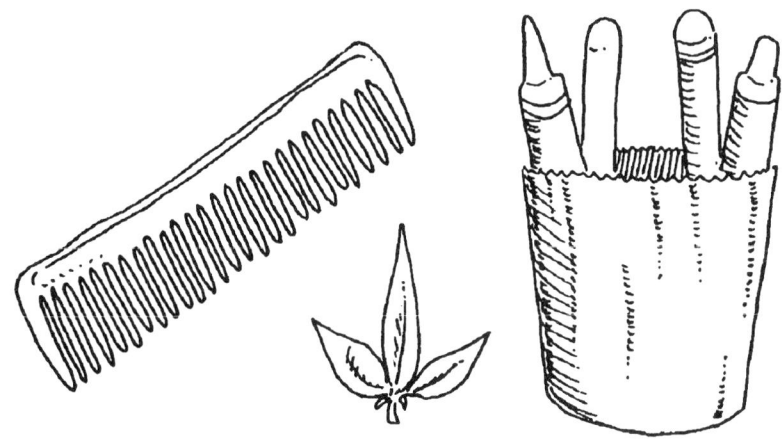

These are great for rubs (see page 6). Put a piece of paper over a comb, penny or leaf and rub gently using the flat side of the melted crayon.

 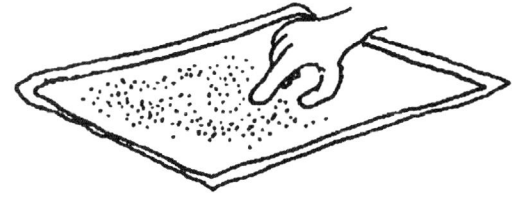

Salt Pictures

Take cookie sheets and cover the bottom with salt. Use your finger or other object, such as a pencil, to draw a picture in the salt. If you make a mistake, or are ready for a new picture, softly shake the cookie sheet and start over!

 Try substituting dry sand for the salt.

Golf Ball Painting

Fill plastic cups with a small amount of paint — each cup containing a different color. Drop a golf ball in each of the cups. Put a piece of paper in the bottom of a roasting pan, or similar size container, and put one or two of the golf balls on top of the paper. Roll the golf balls around by gently moving the pan from side to side. Remove the balls and the paper and allow the paper to dry.

Goopy Bags

Cook a mixture of cornstarch and water on low heat until it thickens. Let it cool completely. Put the mixture in zipper-locking bags and securely tape the top. Let children squeeze the goop to their delight!

For colored goop, add food coloring to the water before cooking.

Fingerprint Creatures

Make fingerprints on a piece of paper using paint or an ink pad. Now try adding heads, legs, arms and tails to your fingerprint body. Once you have created your creature, think of an original name for it.

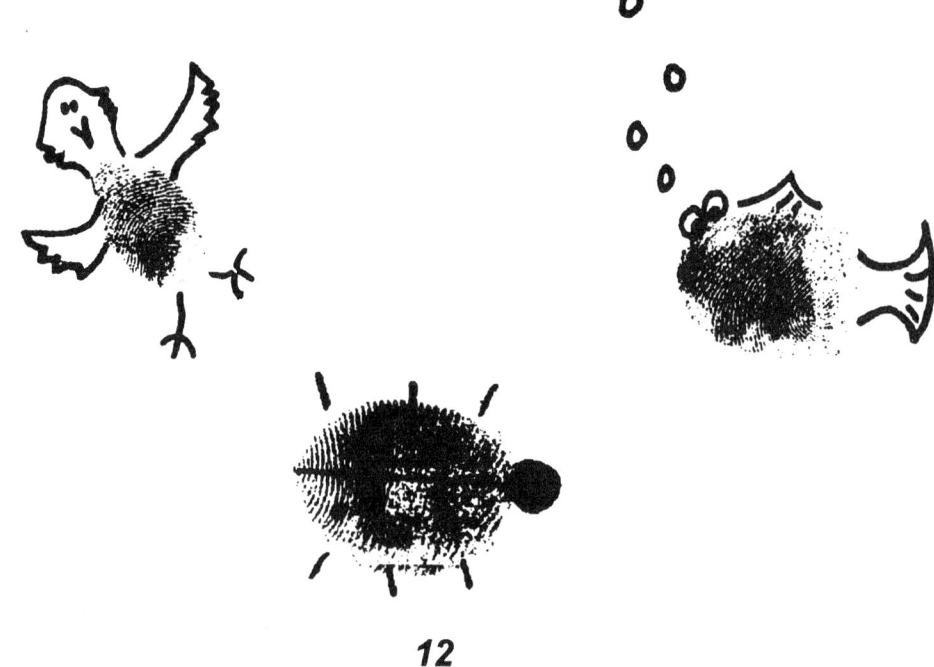

Paper Sculptures

Cut strips of construction paper in different lengths (1" x 8", 1" x 10", and 1" x 12"). Bend each strip every two inches. Tape the ends of each strip to its other end. Use these different shapes to create your very own towers, buildings and other architectural wonders.

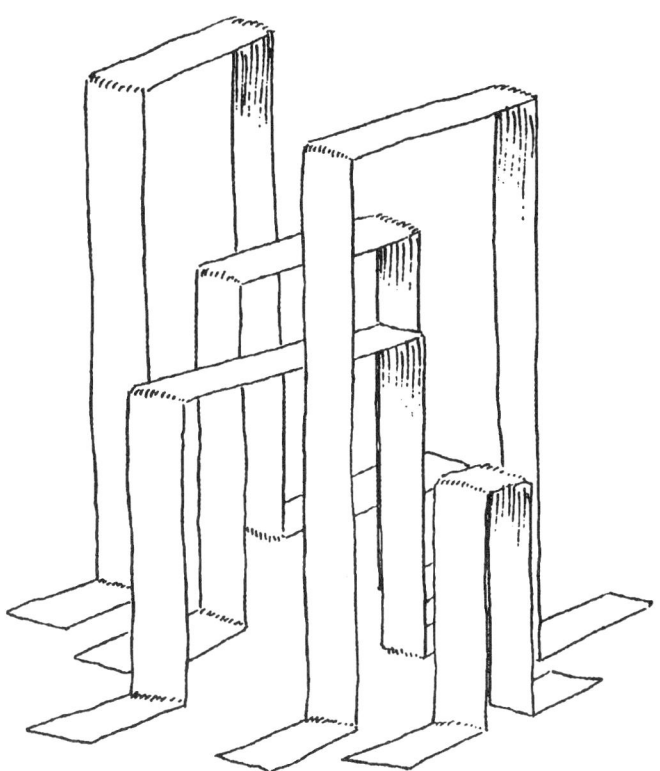

 Vary the widths of the strips for more variety.

Eggshell Pictures

Save one dozen egg shells. Wash and dry them on paper towels. Let children crush them with a rolling pin. Partially fill plastic cups with food coloring and water. Add shells to each of the cups. Let soak for 15 minutes. Dry on a paper towel. Let children arrange and paste shells onto paper in a variety of colors and shapes.

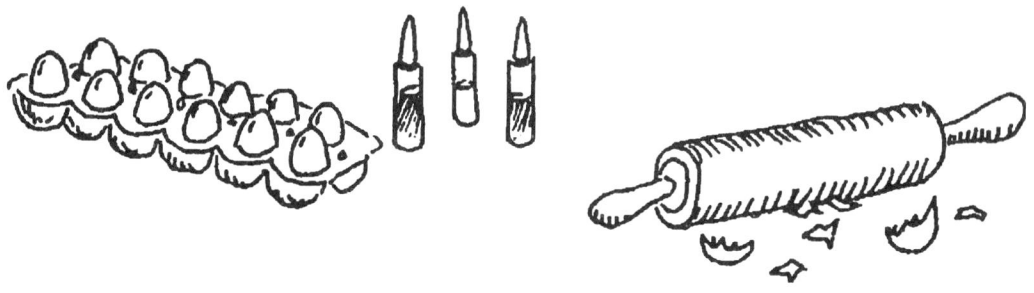

Egg Carton Creatures

Cut out the egg cups from an egg carton. Take two and glue the open sides together to form an oval body shape. Take toothpicks or pipe cleaners and poke four of them into one side of the body to form legs. Use pieces of felt or construction paper to create a face for your creature.

Eyedropper Colors

In separate containers, mix a cup of water with green, yellow, blue, and red food coloring. Fill four compartments of an ice cube tray — each with a different color. Allow children to use an eye dropper and the empty containers of the ice cube tray to make different combinations of the colors to see what new colors they can create.

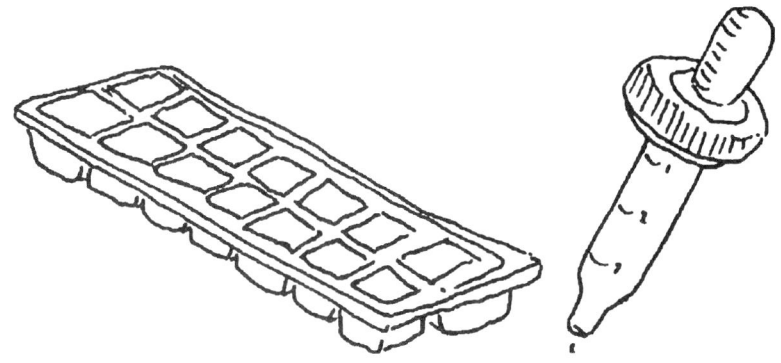

Running Colors

Cut tissue paper into different size circles. Using a water and food coloring mixture such as the one above, drop one small drop of a color on the tissue paper circle. Allow it to soak in and then drop a drop of another color on top. See how the colors run together. Let the circles dry. You may wish to use them to make a colorful collage or as butterfly wings.

Pasta Jewelry

Take dry pasta that has a hole through the middle, and paint it in a variety of colors. Let it dry completely. Thread the pieces randomly or in a pattern by color and shape on a shoelace or cord for your own custom necklace.

The pasta can be varnished (by an adult) for a shiny look.

Glue smaller pasta shapes to the larger one for different looking beads.

These make great gifts for mom and grandma for Mother's Day.

Stenciling

Cut out different shapes from small index cards. Hold this stencil down on top of another piece of paper. Take a sponge dipped in tempera paint and dab it over the cut out on the index card. Lift the card off of the other paper to see the shape left by the stencil and the paint. The stencil cards can be used over and over.

Practice patterns with your stencils. Encourage children to copy a pattern that you have done previously, or to create their own patterns.

Make a picture frame using stencil shapes. Cut out a frame from poster board and use stencils to create your own original art around the edges. Fill the frame with some of your favorite artwork, or a picture of yourself.

Fun Fish Tank

It can be very calming to watch a fish tank, but they can be messy to keep. Make a "no-clean" fish tank by pasting a large (at least 3' x 3') piece of royal blue paper to your wall. Cut some different fish shapes from sturdy colorful paper. Then, using all sorts of different colorful papers — tissue paper, newspaper, wrapping paper, and construction paper — decorate the shapes to create your own colorful fish. Try making a spotted fish with squares of different colored paper, or striped fish with strips of paper.

Rock Animals

Take a walk and collect rocks in different shapes and sizes. See if you can find flat, round, shiny, rough, pointed, and colorful samples.

Bring the rocks back to the classroom and display them on a table for children to choose. You may have some previously created animals on display that will give them ideas for their own sculptures.

Ask children to choose a rock for the animal's body and one for its head. Glue the two rocks together and allow them to dry. Using paint or a marker, draw eyes, a nose, and a mouth on each animal.

Use twisted pipe cleaners or cotton balls to add tails to the animals.

If you want to add feet to your animal, glue smaller pebbles to the bottom of the body.

Worm Farm

Take a large (quart sized) glass jar and alternately layer 1 ½ inches of sand and garden soil until jar is about ¾ full. Add several earthworms that have been dug up from your soil outside. Cover the top of the sand with a layer of rotting leaves. Mist with some water. Cover the jar for several days. Check your jar occasionally to see the tunnels and designs the earthworms have made in the soil.

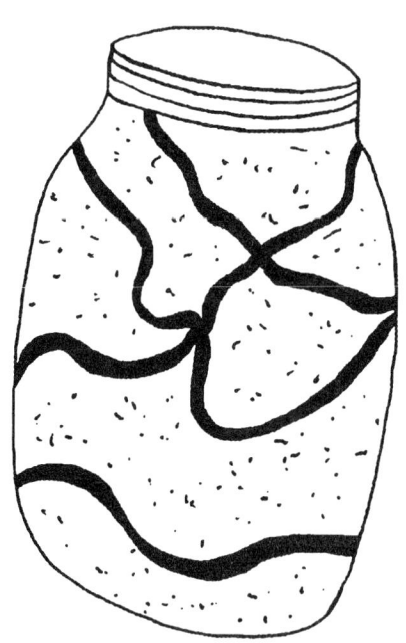

Games

This section contains ideas for games. You may want to play the *Shhh...* CD or audiocassette quietly in the background as you participate in these games.

What's That Smell?

Put small amounts of strong smelling foods in separate containers. Coffee, chocolate, peanut butter, bologna, lemon, bananas, and onions work well. Have children close their eyes, sniff, and try to guess what's in each container.

Try playing "What's That Taste?" Let children sample small tastes of sugar, salt, peanut butter, bread, and so on, with their eyes closed and guess what it is. Assist them by asking if the taste is sweet, salty, smooth, crunchy, etc.

Treasure Hunt

Hide a treasure in your room. Examples of treasures might be healthy snacks; flash cards with letters, colors, or numbers; or a small object that will remind them of something they may be learning in school. Give hints and clues about where the treasure is hiding. Reward them with a sticker for finding the treasure.

Bubbles

Fill a large basin or tub with warm water and add some liquid dish soap. Let children create bubbles using egg beaters, hand mixers, spatulas, measuring cups and other kitchen utensils. Who can make the biggest bubble? Who can hold a bubble the longest?

Bean Bag Toss

Make bean bags from some strong material scraps (e.g., denim, burlap, cotton, etc.). Fill the bags with dry beans.

Cut three or four plastic milk cartons in half and label them 5, 10, 15, and 20 or 1, 2, 3, and 4 for points.

Put a piece of tape on the floor where you would like children to stand to throw the beanbags. Add up everyone's score.

Book Race

Have children try to balance a book on their head and walk quickly, but quietly across the room. This encourages balance and good posture! Try different sized books. What size is easiest to balance? Make sure to pick books that are lightweight so no one's toes get hurt if the book falls.

Can anyone balance two books on top of their head while they walk across the room?

Stick Pickup

Drop popsicle sticks in a small pile on the table or floor. See if children can pick up one stick at a time without touching or moving another stick.

Have children experiment to see if dropping the popsicle sticks from a higher level causes them to scatter farther than dropping them from lower.

Make Believe

While playing the *Shhh...* CD or audiocassette softly in the background, dim the lights and go for a visit to the jungle. Have one person be the tour guide as you quietly sneak around the room looking for imaginary lions and giraffes and other wild jungle animals. Cross a river, swing on a vine, climb a tree, and allow children to really use their imaginations. Next time, try a trip to the top of the highest mountain, or to the hot desert.

Pretend Vacation

Where would you like to go on vacation? Cut out some pictures of places that look interesting to visit and make a travel poster. You can make up the name of your destination, if you wish.

Decide whether you will be driving, riding a bus or train, or flying. Make tickets for your trip.

Pretend that a paper sack or small box is your suitcase and pack the things you'll need on your vacation. Will the destination be warm or cool? What type of clothing will you need?

Arrange chairs or boxes into a row. Pretend this is your airplane, train, bus, or car, and have a great trip!

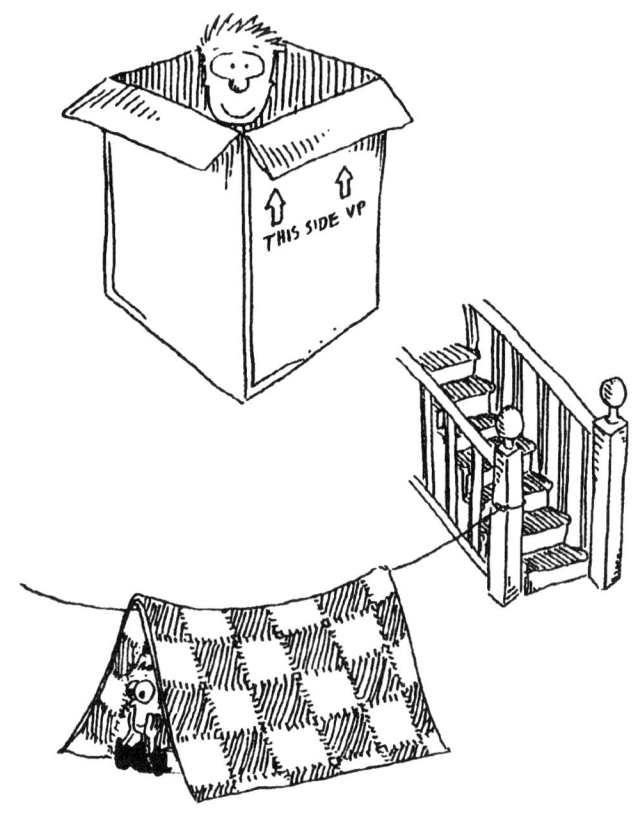

Escape

Children love to escape sometimes into their own little spaces to read or just be alone for awhile. Create ways for them to do this by providing large empty boxes that they can crawl into or areas where they can make a tent out of chairs and old blankets.

Charades

Play a simple game of charades with your children. Write down some situations that would be easy to act out on index cards. Some examples are blowing a bubble, throwing a ball, petting a dog, writing, playing the piano, or driving a car.

Ask who would like to go first and have them pick an index card. Help them read the situation on the card, then encourage them to act it out.

Have the rest of the class guess what the student is acting out.

Popcorn Tray

Fill several holes in an ice cube tray with popcorn. Ask children if they can pick up a piece of popcorn with a pair of tweezers and move it to another hole in the tray. Try arranging popcorn on just one side, or skip a hole each time, or fill every hole and ask them to remove them all. This is great for fine motor development.

Heavier objects such as buttons can also be used, but are a little harder to manipulate.

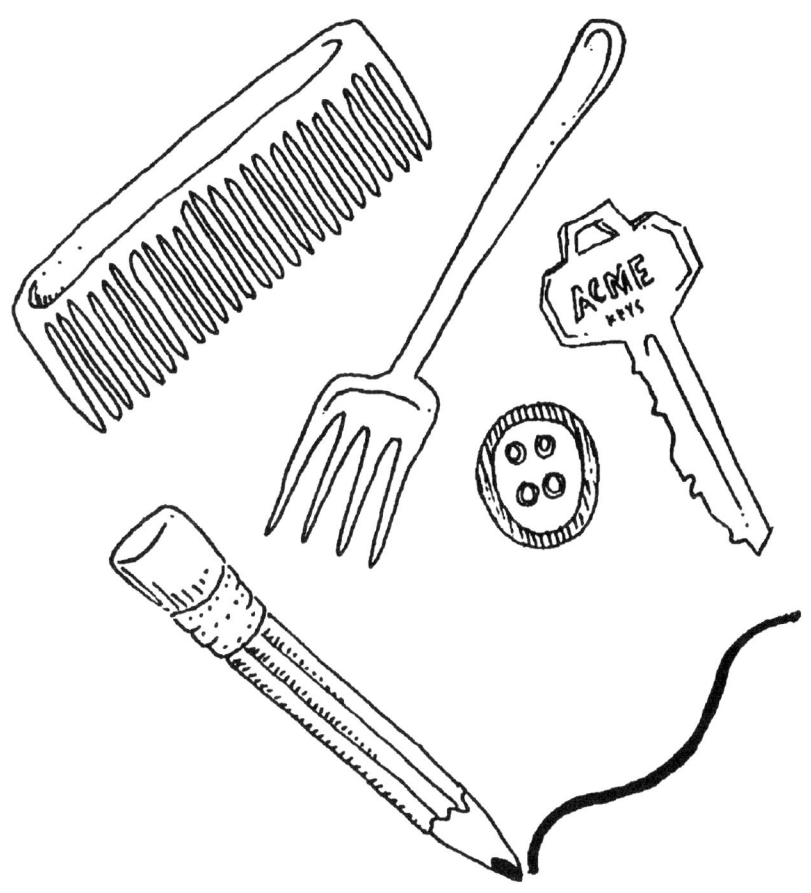

Tell Me What's Missing

Arrange several objects such as a key, button, fork, pencil and comb on a tray. The older the child, the more objects you can use. Have children study the tray and when they are ready, close their eyes. Remove one object from the tray, then have them open their eyes and guess which object is missing.

Musical Cards

Instead of musical chairs, try playing musical letters, colors or numbers. Make playing cards out of 8½ x 11 inch colored construction paper. On one side of each card, print a letter or a number. If possible, laminate each card to prevent tearing when children step on them, but be careful because this may make them slippery when placed on certain surfaces.

Make a large circle of cards on a non-slip floor using the same number of cards as the number of children playing.

Play the music and have children walk, skip, jump, walk backwards, and so on around the circle of cards. When the music stops, have each child identify the number, color or letter he is standing on. If they have difficulty identifying what is on their card, have everyone say it together.

With older children, try using pictures of animals, easy math problems, or even state capitals!

Where's the Quarter?

Have children sit on the floor in a circle. Ask the child who is the first leader to step out of the room. Give the quarter to one of the children in the circle and have them sit on it.

Ask the leader to come back into the room and have all the children in the circle hum a well-known song with you, such as "Twinkle Twinkle Little Star." As the leader gets closer to the person sitting on the quarter, hum louder. When the leader moves farther away, hum softer. Continue until the leader has identified the child who is sitting on the quarter.

Choose another leader and try it again!

Movement Activities

This section contains ideas for quiet time movement activities. You may want to play the *Shhh...* CD or audiocassette quietly in the background as you participate in these activities.

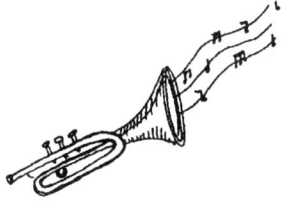

Free Movement

Turn the lights down low and encourage children to move in a way that sounds like the music (e.g., soft, slow, smooth, etc.). Assist them in thinking of movements that fit the music. If your children tend to pick fast, abrupt movements when given free movement, play a very active, moving piece of music (e.g., ragtime, country, rock, and so on). What are the differences between the quiet time music and the faster paced music? Have them move to the faster music, then switch to the slower. Model suggested movements for them.

Balloon Play

Inflate some large balloons and ask children to make them float. Encourage children not to hit the balloons, but to touch them as if their fingers were sharp pins — very softly and carefully! Remember that deflated balloons can be a choking hazard, so immediately discard broken balloons and keep deflated balloons in a safe place.

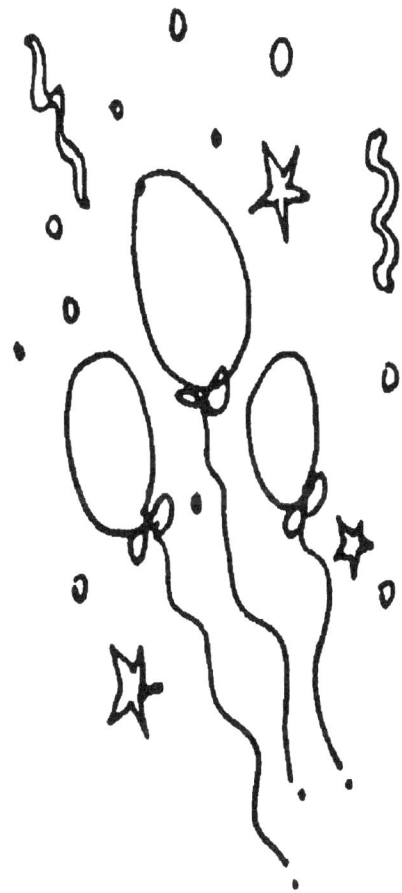

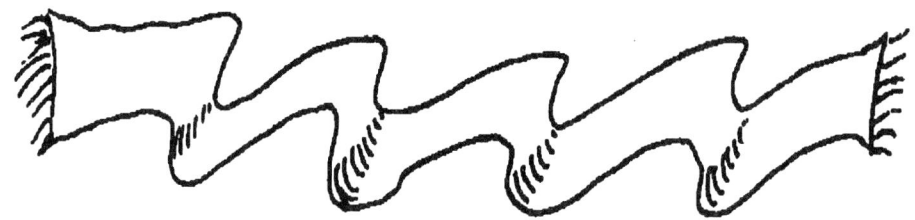

Scarf Dancing

Provide children with colorful scarves or pieces of cloth in a variety of fabrics and textures (silky, gauzy, heavy, light). With soft music playing in the background, encourage children to move with their scarves and let the scarves flutter and fly in the breeze.

Mirroring

Have children sit in a way that they can all see you. Using your hands and upper body, have children mirror your actions. Tell them to pretend that they are looking in a mirror and ask them to move just like you are. Start with very small deliberate motions, and work up to larger sweeping motions.

 Ask if anyone else would like to be the mirror!

Exploring Body Planes

While calming music plays in the background, have children lay on their backs on the floor. Encourage them to explore all the different ways their arms and legs can move while laying in that position. Switch positions. Have them try laying on their stomachs, kneeling on their hands and knees, laying on one side, standing up, and so on. How do their arms and legs move differently in each position?

Footprints

Try to find footprints sold as stick-on or non-skid bathtub decals. Or, cut 20—30 out of construction paper. Paper footprints will need to be taped to the floor as they can slip when stepped on. Place these in a pattern that can be followed by children as soft music plays. Once the first pattern has been mastered by all, rearrange the footprints into a slightly more difficult pattern.

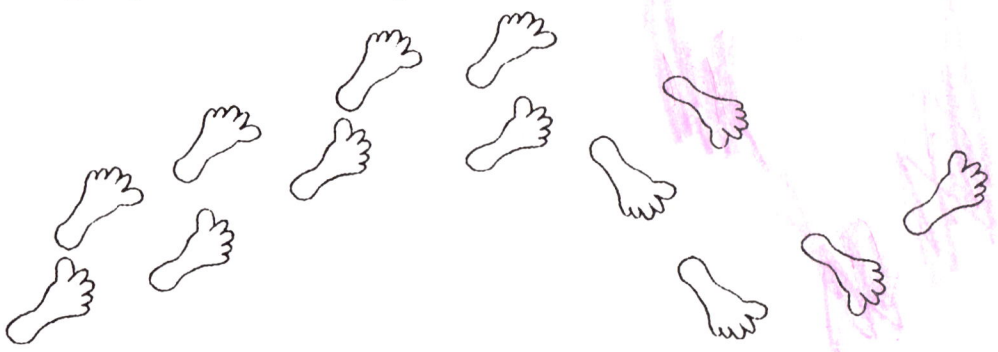

38

Science Activities

This section contains ideas for science activities. You may want to play the *Shhh...* CD or audiocassette quietly in the background as you participate in these activities.

Salt Garden

4 tbsp. salt
1 tbsp. ammonia
4 tbsp. water
2 or 3 charcoal briquets
food coloring

Break up the pieces of charcoal and place in a bowl. Mix ammonia, water, and salt, and pour the mixture over the charcoal. Put drops of food coloring on the charcoal. Crystals will grow on charcoal in 1—2 days.

Egg Faces

Empty egg shells with top ¼ gently cracked off
Napkin ring or something else to hold the egg upright
Cotton balls
Alfalfa seeds
Markers

Set eggshell in a napkin ring, or other holder. Carefully draw a face on the egg with magic markers. Place several damp cotton balls in each egg. Sprinkle alfalfa seeds over the cotton balls and keep them damp. Seeds will begin to sprout in several days.

Drinking Celery

Cut the bottoms off of several stalks of celery. Put the celery in a glass of water that is half full. Add several drops of food coloring to the water. After several hours, take the celery out of the water and break it or cut it in slices. See how far the water has traveled up the stalk. Leave one stalk in the water overnight and then compare the two.

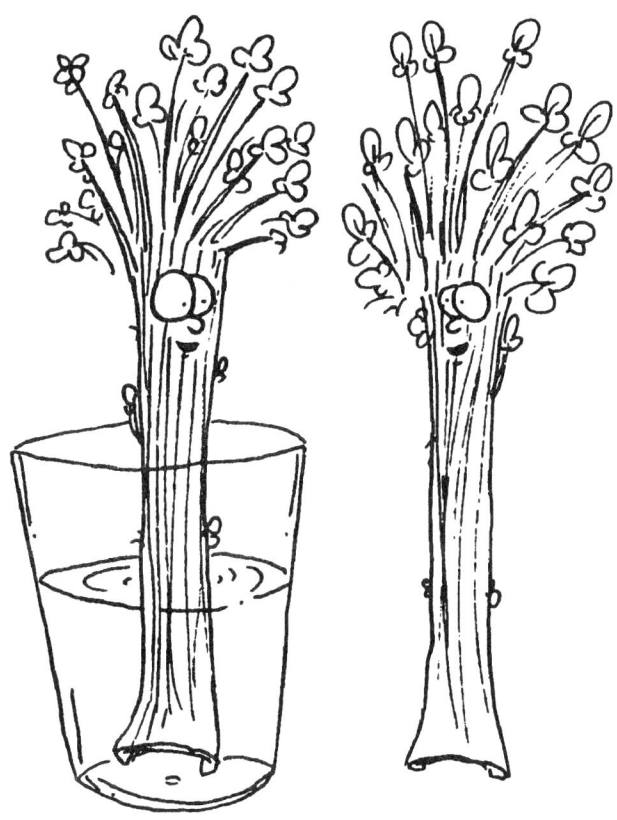

 This is also fun to try with a white carnation!

Quiet Time Music

Highland Mist

by Pamela Ott

Sunset Embrace

by Pamela Ott

Lambs Are Sleeping

traditional
arranged by Pamela Ott

49

Dawn's Awakening

by Pamela Ott

Brahms Lullaby

by Johannes Brahms
arranged by Pamela Ott

Inspiration

by Pamela Ott

Till We Meet Again

by Pamela Ott

60

Evening Star

by Richard Wagner
arranged by Pamela Ott

61

When You're There

by Pamela Ott

65

Small Wonder

by Pamela Ott

Cricket Serenade

by Pamela Ott

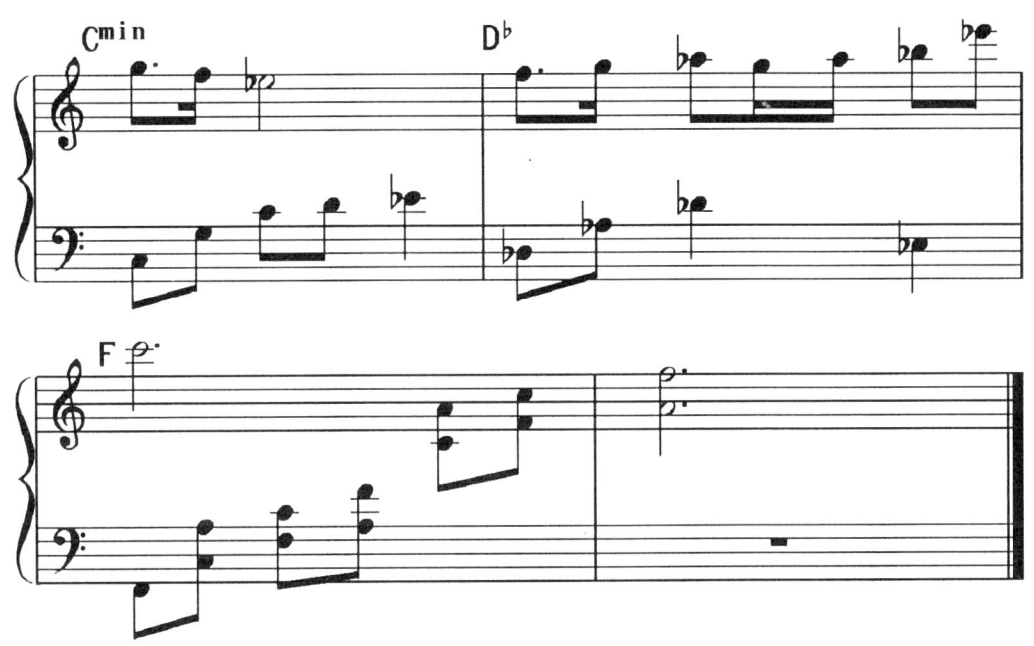

71

Man in the Moon

by Pamela Ott

73

Sleepytime

traditional
arranged by Pamela Ott

Paint the Desert

by Pamela Ott

78

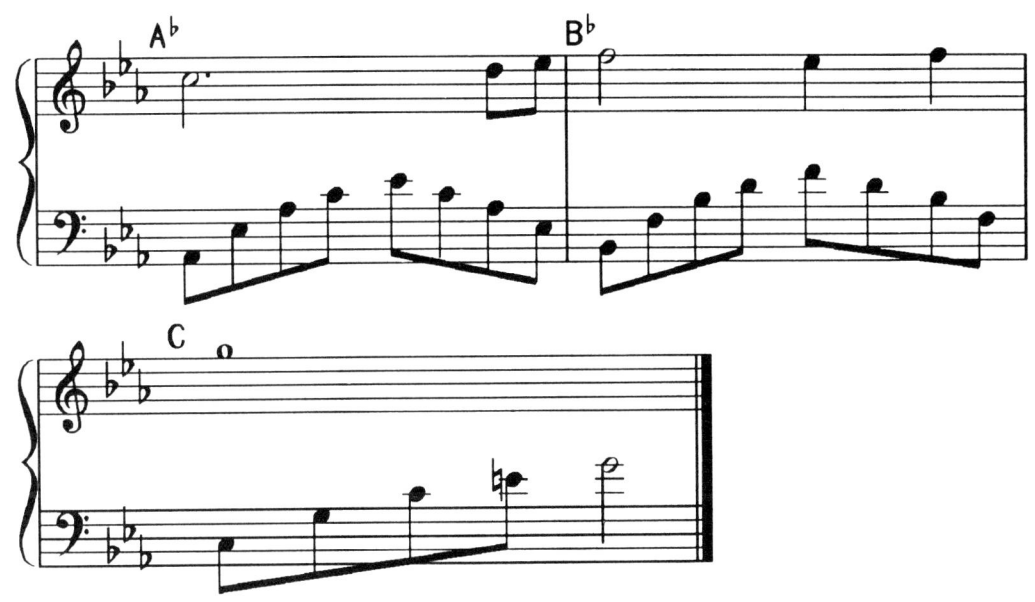

Sweet Dreams

by Pamela Ott

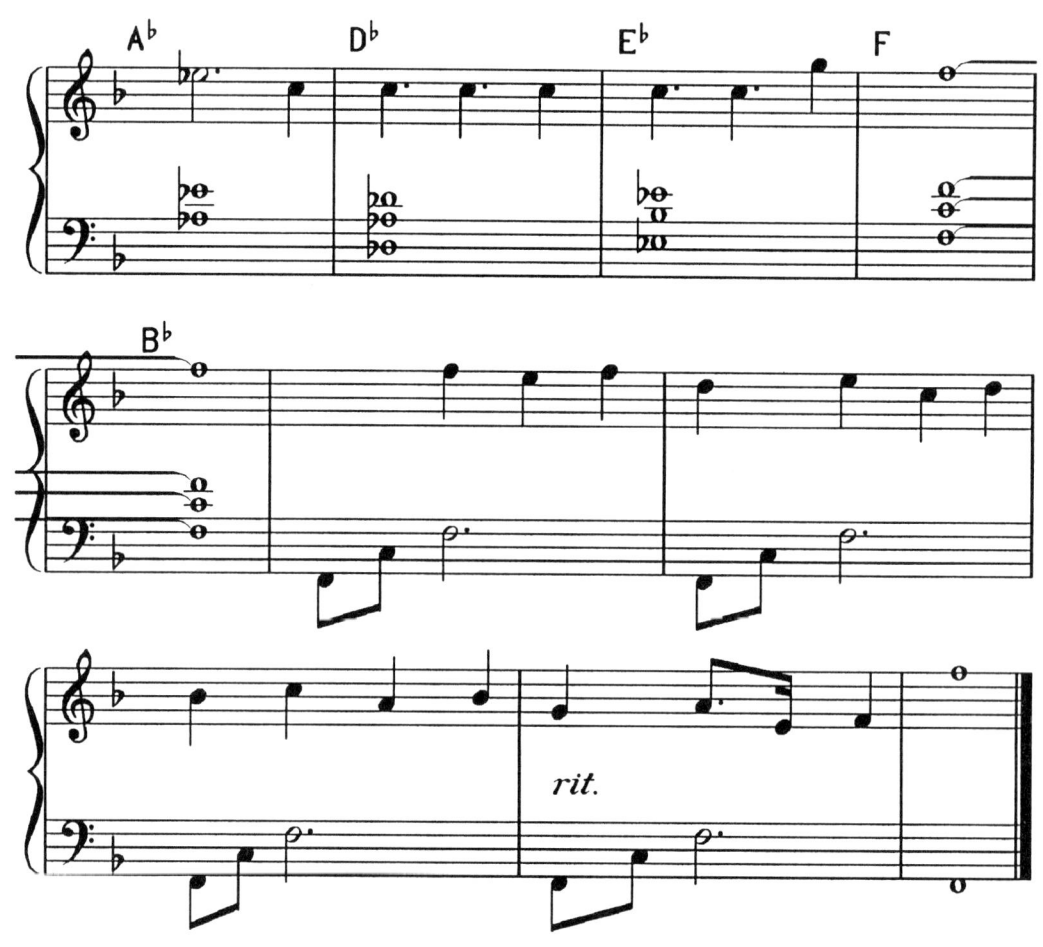

Index